ENEMY
ON THE WAY
TO SCHOOL

Annette Hayn
With a Foreword by Mary Ferrari
Illustrations by Deborah Hayn

THE POET'S PRESS
Pittsburgh, PA

This is the 166th publication of
THE POET'S PRESS
2209 Murray Avenue #3
Pittsburgh, PA 15217-2338

CONTENTS

FOREWORD

I have long hoped that Annette Hayn would collect, in one volume, her poems primarily written about her childhood in Nazi Germany. I am delighted that now, in this book, she has done it. The extraordinary poems presented here have an at times overwhelming cumulative power. They recapture a happy childhood in Germany, as it is gradually overshadowed by confusion and fear.

Written over a thirty-year period, some of the poems have been previously published in poetry magazines and in earlier collections of Annette's work. She is a highly accomplished poet who is a recipient of the Bernice Kavinoky Isaacson Award for poetry at the New School. Frances Waldman praised the intellectual rigor of her poetry. It is remarkable that most of her poems about the Holocaust are unsentimental and concise.

The title, *Enemy on the Way to School,* from her poem, "A Song," is aptly paradoxical: as if a child on the way to school could be the enemy. "School," as used here, evokes for me a second education: learning what it means to be an innocent enemy, an appropriate oxymoron describing her situation; and later on, what it means to be an adolescent enabled to escape from the worst that Hitler had to offer her and her parents' generation of Jews.

Annette's early love of the theatre and of acting provides a dramatic metaphor for the terrifying aspects of her youthful experience. "Aria," the first poem, is brief; the scene is Verdi's *Othello.* In the contrast between the "row of shadows/ against the wall/..." and Desdemona's acceptance of her fate "in bold circles of color," Annette's childhood persona seems to be absorbing two ways to meet the growing emergency: as an anonymous victim or as a heroine.

"Where Dragons Sang" is a wonderful poem that begins with a dreamlike sequence: "What I remember has/ no beginning and no walls/ each fragment hangs like a cloud...". Annette practices the piano as a domestic image disappears: "a crystal chandelier/ falls from the cloud/ slowly it keeps on/ falling like snow—/." In the third section, her stream of consciousness technique reflects perfectly the child's emerging consciousness of distressing events. Her memory "walks backwards," beginning with happy or ambiguous images and ending with terror:

> Now I'm walking backwards on
> this German avenue (I feel quite
> safe) in boots, under a narrow
> moon, past the mysterious fire
> walking to where my mother
> knew I loved her
> to where the Stürmer printed
> lies on giant columns on every
> street—a Jew with crooked nose and
> evil eyes. some boys
> cornered me—

Annette's governess is one of the heroines of these poems. In "Kinderfräulein," Annette writes matter-of-factly, "Lisbeth stayed loyal to the Jews/ although it was forbidden." Lisbeth takes Annette to her village where there is a frightening occurrence: One morning churchbells rang/ "for clergymen/ in concentration camps./ That puts us all in danger." "Kinderfräulein" ends with a paradoxical double vision:

> The village was too poor
> for postcards of itself, too small
> to be discovered. When the Nazis neared
> the roofs left the horizon
>
> and Lisbeth unchanged.

The village, too small to be discovered, ironically is. These last lines sound as if "the roofs left the horizon," as if Lisbeth remains the one continuum.

Annette's mother is the other heroine of her childhood and of these poems, as Annette explains in "The Ascent." Her mother is a mountain climber whom Annette admires above everyone else. Her mountain climbing is both real and metaphorical, and, to her small daughter, she is sometimes out of reach:

> From the base
> of an Italian mountain
> I looked up
> trying to locate her.

Later, she cites her mother's bravery:

> She bribed the girlfriend
> of a camp commander
> to release my father
> then almost didn't
> get away herself.

In contrast, "Drawings by Max Liebermann" is a poem in part "about" her father from whom she felt a youthful detachment. Her father was a lawyer and art collector. As in Annette's poems about the theatre, the drawings by Max Liebermann take on another life as political metaphors:

> The Germans burned Liebermann's works
> but the people with no faces
> in his drawings
> the horses waves and trees
> galloped away

The subjects of the drawings manage to escape, as does Annette. Time moves back and forth in this discursive poem, encompassing Annette's changing attitude toward her father, the changing attitude in Germany toward Liebermann's works, as well as Annette's changing attitude toward them. A drawing of small girls develops a personal resonance: "unframed for forty years"—as if they are the small Jewish girls suddenly disappearing from each other's lives. Now in writing about them, she gives them a double frame: they stay still at the beginning of their lives, as they look forward to a normal "starting out."

"White Flowers" is a brief, startling pastoral that begins:

Edelweiss was Hitler's favorite flower.

Climbers in the poem appear to be Hitler's henchmen, risking their lives to pick edelweiss, but also making arbitrary decisions about the lives and deaths of people, innocent as white flowers: "press this one throw/ away that/...".

"Idols" recreates the excitement of the theatre, as well as the counterpoint of the tragic drama going on in Berlin: the denouement for the Jewish artists, who nonetheless act "like super heroes;" for Amelia, who "sang Verdi's score/ as they tore off her veil/..."; and, for the audience as well in a "last theatre:"

dim lights, the painted gallows
all of us elegant and doomed
in A Masked Ball

Wrapped in applause and awe
next to my mother, small
I watched them disappear
in all directions

Disappearance is a natural theme in these elegiac poems. "The Children of Kings" is inspired by one of Annette's favorite childhood songs, "Königskinder;" the song enlarges Annette's reality, as it dramatizes the disappearance of children, including implicitly herself:

The water was too deep. Over and over
the *Königskinder*
drowned in my favorite song,
I watched them disappear/...

"The Children of Kings" seems to reflect, too, Annette's sense of the tenuousness of her own privileged position.

Annette's own disappearance took a comparatively benign form. She spent the years 1937 to 1940 in England, as a refugee in a boarding school at Brighton. "The Island," one of the poems that focuses on this period, is the masterpiece in this collection. A beautiful poem based on a verse-form used by Goethe; its rhyme and repetition give a formal order to an emotionally disordered time. The island seems to be both England and a metaphor for an isolated state of mind. The effort to grow up normally under abnormal circumstances seems to be a continuation of Annette's earlier attempt to go on having a happy childhood despite the Nazi menace. Annette and her fellow students enjoyed the pleasures of adolescence as they endured anxiety about the fates of parents forced to remain behind. "The Island" is wonderfully evocative, rising and falling in tone and image like the waves, actual and emotional, that surround it, as in the first stanza:

First formal dance in England:
We fell in love in quicksand.
Too young to take a stand
We smiled and closed our eyes.

I especially admire the poignant paradox of the second line: that the pleasure of falling in love should be combined with the fear of sinking into the figurative quicksand of the Holocaust, and, so concisely in one line!

"The Island" is followed by "The Crossing," an historically transitional poem, recording Annette's second and final displacement: from England to the U.S. in 1940. Lighter in tone, "The Crossing" begins with a humorous recollection of a compliment from a Norwegian sailor during a blackout: "I like your teeth;" continues with an odd complaint about being "rescued by ship;" and concludes with an acceptance of "zigzagging to the other side/ of my life."

Elizabeth Bishop said that she only wanted to write about things that really happened. (Millier, *Elizabeth Bishop*) Annette's poems in *Enemy on the Way to School*, despite surrealistic imagery, are exemplary descendants in this realist tradition. Personal, not didactic, these poems make no direct political commentaries on the Holocaust. Each poem presented here, from the most beautiful and overwhelming to the slightest, is based on a concrete scene, a fragment of remembered conversation, an event. They are political only in the personal sense that Anne Frank's "Diary" is.

Annette's prose poem, "Turandot," for instance, emphasizes her youthful excitement at winning the part of a remarkable slave girl, Zelima, in Schiller's play, and her delight in constant rehearsing. "Turandot" ends tersely:

> But the play was written by a German poet and was not to be performed by Jewish children. It was forbidden.
> *Turandot* did not take place.

Annette makes no reference to her disappointment which must have been crushing. Her enthusiasm for the theatre and for acting are central. The Nazis were obviously having a terrible effect on her life, as well as on the lives of thousands of others. She treats this fact with ironic detachment. Art paradoxically created out of loss is one valid definition of outstanding poetry. Annette Hayn's *Enemy on the Way to School* provides a luminous example.

Mary Ferrari
April 25, 1994
Johannesburg

ENEMY
ON THE WAY
TO SCHOOL

*I would like to thank Mary Ferrari
for her encouragement and help.*

For Jessica, Andrew, Erik,
Daniel and Rebecca.

*...I have not seen a single cemetery flower
in so happy a procession of lights.
Forgive me, Lord! I have died so little!...*

*César Vallejo
from Agape
translated by John Knoepfle*

ARIA

during Desdemona's *Ave Maria*
I saw the row of shadows
against the wall
raised my hand afraid
of anonymity
to find out which one of them
was me while Desdemona
prepared for death
in bold circles of color.

WHERE DRAGONS SANG

1

What I remember has
no beginning and no walls.
each fragment hangs like a cloud
without a sky. slowly
as I practice the
piano, a crystal chandelier
falls from the cloud
slowly it keeps on
falling like snow—

2

I can recall
a door that didn't open
a child I wouldn't
play with, the play I missed
not what I kept on seeing
through the window
(blue out of nowhere, suns
out of sequence) thinking
I'll always remember this

the door was on a mountain
the play about a virgin
who chopped off someone's head—
when the carriage overturned
the child I wouldn't play with
picked up my four dolls
from the grass spitefully
left me an evil image of myself.

3
Now I'm walking backwards on
this German avenue (I feel quite
safe) in boots under a narrow
moon, past the mysterious fire
walking to where my mother
knew I loved her
to where the Stürmer printed
lies on giant columns on every
street — a Jew with crooked nose and
evil eyes. some boys
cornered me —
walking to where our dog hid from
the birthday party where dragons sang
and shadows carried guns
to where the *Nibelungen*,
the wronged dwarfs—

I stepped on the white berry
made a popping sound. the lady in the
moss house drifted down the river.
I held four dolls. Siegfried revived
his dragon. the streetsigns marched
saluted, turned around..

THE GAME

Edith and I, the only
girls in the battle. Flushed,
out of breath, we piled snow bullets
on a sled while our mothers
looked for us all over Breslau.

Another time
we threw our dolls downhill
to see if they could fly (they did
for a moment)
but hers was made of porcelain
and had to have new eyes.

It was all a game:
the enemies in boots parading
down the street, fathers
losing their jobs, getting arrested.
But that came afterwards. First

we were six —
Nazis and Jews together
in a garden. I can't remember
who was who
— flinging snow bullets
at enemies across the fence
until the sun went down
and our mothers found us.

Surrounded by the
greenery that was
my life I overheard two men
"impending misfortune
for all of us" they said
"since Hindenburg has died"
and it meant nothing
to me (why do I remember)
meant nothing on a balcony
of the Riesengebirge
the middle of —
and it meant no
more than a story
I wasn't in.

A SONG

We played by the river
gave it two letters from each
of our names so it became
Evanlireha Bach

Lisbeth made up a song about the river
We built islands for creatures
with tree bark eyes. Italian
soldiers on maneuvers
used them for their tents

That was before the cook
was married and the dog grew lonely
before we moved from Breslau to Berlin

Soldiers stole rocks from our dam, opened
flood gates — Back home
men streamed
in mud brown uniforms
through the streets
and sang *Die Fahne hoch* —

I was proud to be the enemy
on my way to school.

THE CHILDREN OF KINGS

The water was too deep. Over and over
the Königskinder
drowned in my favorite song.
I watched them disappear

Lisbeth my governess was there
on all the continents
train tracks past fortune tellers
with dark painted faces

When I was frightened she made up
verses for me to recite
replaced the doll's eye. I could do anything
(Lisbeth inside my head)

A sign said *Danger, keep away!*
Hundreds of fleeing feet.
In the song
the Königskinder drowned again —

In love on separate shores
they tried to reach
one another—
The water was too deep

Across the border I got dizzy
in a blue limelight
in carousels
in the Lieder she used to sing to me.

THE WOODS

Snow-covered   secretive
the trees gathered on the edges
of reality
where witches carried flags
haunted railroad tracks
and I ran from a butterfly
that grew and grew —

Some nights I followed
Hansel and Gretel into the woods

TO KEEP YOUR BALANCE

the secret is
don't be afraid and keep
your balance—

will there be snow?
is the hour waiting in a brass bed
half way up the mountain will these footsteps
come in?

round and round I rode a bicycle —
the village had to get out of my way
I couldn't stop
till Lisbeth entered the circle
to rescue me

that's how I learned to fall
in love with shadows from
the sleeping houses
and learned to fall
on skis before I knew
another way of slowing down

KINDERFRÄULEIN

Lisbeth stayed loyal to the Jews
although it was forbidden. She made
sailboats out of newspaper
and took me to her village.

At first the village
was invisible.
Outhouses, chickens, fields
a bed took shape. Nothing was lit.

One morning churchbells rang
"for clergymen
in concentration camps.
That puts us all in danger."

The village was too poor
for postcards of itself, too small
to be discovered.
When the Nazis neared
the roofs left the horizon

and Lisbeth unchanged.

Those drawings turned
their backs to me. I wandered
past them every day.
Just lines
without a story

I didn't wish to grow up
like my father
a lawyer art collector.
Only the paintings of battles
appealed to me
in noisy reds

But in the drawings
everything is open to interpretation.
I didn't know
some of the lines and curves
are boys undressing
on a beach

It was a matter of each other's territory:
The singer I had a crush on
didn't exist
for my father

As I grew older
loved my father better
the Germans burned Liebermann's works

but the people with no faces
in his drawings
the horses waves and trees
galloped away

Now they reemerge. No one
in these sketches
stays put. Germany reclaims
Max Liebermann. My father
dies. The pencil lines fade in and out
like new events —

Meanwhile I have rehung
a study of small girls
I had forgotten and never liked

girls squatting down
unframed for forty years
their shaded knees, and girls in laps
just starting out.

POSTMARK

Sometimes the sun
seemed like a postmark
in the sky. I thought
the light from our kitchen
window was bullet proof. robots
with swastikas sang the
Horst Wessel Lied. "it won't
get any worse" my father said.

Schiller's version of St. Joan
fallen in battle
covered with flags

Horizon of enemies in Berlin
enemies marching
the breaking of wills

In a courtyard in a dream
I fight the enemy
and hold a flag

The one
who holds a flag
is always right

Then the
remaining flags
are lowered softly

FROM ZONE TO ZONE

I rode on the
pine needle surface of
the *Grunewald.* some
of the buildings
were later bombed, weed trees
reaching through roofs —
we played polo on bicycles
on shifting sandy surfaces
that sometimes caught a wheel
made us fall
the sinking surface of
my mother's bed, slippery
surfaces around the school,
soft snow that rocked
us falsely —
bicycling in and out
from zone to zone
of clouds on cobblestone.

THE ASCENT

(for my mother)

From the base
of an Italian mountain
I looked up
trying to locate her

"Take me along"   shadows
climbing way up high
"Later   when you're older"

My father knew
the Roman emperors
but not the Nazi mind
She made our decisions

Her reddish hair
tied back for the ascent
a reddish sun
glued to a cliff
the mountain almost
perpendicular

She bribed the girlfriend
of a camp commander
to release my father
then almost didn't
get away herself

Tied to each other
the climbers turned
to dots above my eyes

Edelweiss was Hitler's favorite flower.
To find it climbers risked
their lives — press this one   throw
away that

I was told to pick daisies
while Lisbeth walked away
        with her fiancé
who she said was her brother

On a meadow in Italy
the aunt—who committed suicide
to escape the Nazis—was afraid of cows.

In Berlin in 1936 something miraculous happened. I landed a part in a play, the part of Zelima, one of the slaves in Schiller's *Turandot*. I was not an ordinary slave like the ones who bowed low before the Kaiser and then crouched in the background or those who danced or those who played the drums. I had words to say on three different occasions though not as many as Adelma, the wicked slave who was a former princess. I was to wear a Chinese costume with one braid. The play was directed by the sarcastic teacher with a crooked smile whom I admired, and we rehearsed for six months.

At home I talked of nothing else. My parents became thoroughly bored. To extend my horizons they took me to the *Kulturbund* where Jewish actors and singers fired by German theaters put on their own performances. The theater was gay and festive. With their lives in jeopardy the artists took on other lives: became Prince Orlofsky, Amelia and Faust. Those others took over the halls. I remember meeting them in the tall mirrors, on the upholstered chairs.

That winter I broke my wrist while skiing. Although my mother wanted me to take time off from school I couldn't wait to resume rehearsals and practiced bowing down, my forehead to the ground, with a cast on. But the play was written by a German poet and was not to be performed by Jewish children. It was forbidden. *Turandot* did not take place.

RELIGION

In Rilke's story
the children lose a thimble —
(I like the way it sometimes
glows in the night.)

Hitler decides: *Death
to the Jews.*
Some Jewish children are baptized
(to keep them safe) or sent away.

A stranger says, "What are you
searching for?"
The child says, "God."

The stranger answers, "Never mind.
Look at this beautiful thimble
I found today."

MARIANNE

Years later I came across her
German letters, assertive, questioning
written in '37
after six months of strolling:
a Berlin schoolyard, arm in arm.

Striving for some storybook
perfection we sent our lives
from Italy to England and
back again. There was that singer,
unrequited love, "quite normal at
our age," she said

remembering how we had once waited
for hours in a hallway
across the street from Dr. Löwenthal,
the teacher we had a crush on
who never got away.

Politics were, like paintings
in our houses, important only when
one looked at them. We looked
at new lights on the edge of seas.
One day all those events
will step out of their frames.
Married one day we won't know
each other's names.

IDOLS

Branches tremble —
a sky white, hot and far away
as in the vestibule of mirrors

perfume in the air
Kulturbund in Berlin in '36

Jewish artists (I had a crush
on one of them) in their
last theater
performing melodramas
from yet another time

confident, like super heroes —
In a green gown
Amelia sang Verdi's score
as they tore off her veil

(groups of Nazis in the street)

dim lights, the painted gallows
all of us elegant and doomed
in *A Masked Ball*

Wrapped in applause and awe
next to my mother, small
I watched them disappear
in all directions

Nothing could touch me then
till I was sent away
into a strangeness that was safe.

Pitt fell in trying to jump the ditch.
The cook made love to him. He never
took to children, but Lisbeth made me
paper boats that sailed away
past bridges and moss houses until
the soldiers came, took
everything, our river.

The village all unlighted from the train,
a hot brick in my bed.
They had never met
a Jew or anybody from the city,
but I could ride on a bicycle
to where they sold postcards,
and I named the goats.

I was the moment between going up
and coming down when I was
seven and afraid
of fortune tellers. We played polo
on bicycles and I got stuck in the sand.

My aunt tucked me in. She was nothing
but a good wife, when I was Joan of Arc
and all the bugs had souls that died
or were sent away.

...   ...

INTRODUCTION

(Brighton, England)

Regardless of what's playing
every Saturday
I do not understand the language
but look forward to it anyway —
the movie theater, a safe retreat.

In this English boarding school
we deal with homesick shadows.
I don't like to be
a rescued refugee — with my mother
sailing back into the storm.

In between shows we play
cricket against other schools,
witness a turbulent sea
from the safety of cliffs,
walk in and out of stories.

Bette Davis stars in *Jezebel.*
A war begins.
From an invaded window
someone pours boiling water
on passing troops.

BOARDING SCHOOL

(England 1938)

Barricaded now behind new doors
in another country
what made us indestructible?

Remember ripping the lining
out of a steel hat
or darting straight up
into that storm
while walking through the park
in uniform   in line —

At the crossroads
dressed alike
during the coronation
of King George

"You may chew in the street
where you come from
but never here in England"
Mock Parliament of foreign children
during the coronation
of King George

All morning I'm Joan of Arc
A teacher who was fired
winks at me and wanders on
during the coronation
of King George

Two by two we pass by rows of roses
cloaks of rain
rumors of parents
in concentration camps
during the coronation of King George

Across the ocean our other lives —
No one must talk
in line or walk alone
during the coronation
of King George.

IN JULIET'S CAPE

German children in white straw hats
in a mock Parliament
beyond the holocaust

Safe on a stage in Juliet's cape
I saw them from the window
of the love scene, led away —

Cloud through the lighted bells
cloud through the red balloon

THE ISLAND

First formal dance in England:
We fell in love in quicksand.
Too young to take a stand
We smiled and closed our eyes.

Too young to take a stand
We saw sharks in disguise
And ships that tried to land.
We smiled and closed our eyes.

And ships that tried to land
Were taken by surprise.
Ghosts led us by the hand
Said, smile and close your eyes.

Ghosts led us by the hand
Grownups who once seemed wise.
Their murders were preplanned.
Just smile and close your eyes.

Their murders were preplanned.
Tucked in on an island
We grew up in quicksand
And smiled and closed our eyes.

THE CROSSING

(from England to the U.S.)

I like your teeth
said a Norwegian sailor
under the British flag
during the blackout.
    but I grew up

in Germany
    Schiller's heroes
    Hitler's jails
and didn't want to be

rescued by ship
    shadowy moon behind
    eleven passengers
zigzagging to the other side
of my life.

POSTSCRIPT —
YEARS LATER

THE PAINTED MOUNTAIN

the mountain was painted in Italy
the one I never got to climb

the painted mountain
after a storm
patches of edelweiss like moons

the mountain of the cat
filled with books
the mountain in the opera
with stairs

the mountains were invisible
in Switzerland on our honeymoon
we looked for cows with bells on
in a downpour

mountain where Joan of Arc
conversed with angels
and dispersed her sheep

mountain where Wilhelm Tell
defied the governor
mountain where the Valkyries
carried fallen warriors

so easily the lights go out
the painted mountain
out of reach

FAMILY PHOTOGRAPH

They told me my grandfather
had died before I was born
but now I find
a photograph
of him and me
in Germany
in the same time zone
in the front row —
one of us does not belong
my grandfather
(a ghost on a visit?)
or I, cross legged
on the floor —
in the shadow of
a falling empire
we haunt each other

Lotte and Liesel
Former Berlin classmates
Walked back into my life—
Years ago the class ignored
A boring teacher, pretended
To be asleep.

Catching up on her sleep
On my sofa, an aging Liesel
(I can't pretend
To recognize this classmate)
Remembering me who had ignored
That period of my life.

In my new life
Of forgetful days and sleep
I have ignored
Lotte and Liesel,
The classmates
Who grew up never pretending.

But I have pretended
All my life.
I've imagined my classmates
Safely sleepwalking
(A Lotte and a Liesel
Among them, anonymous, ignored.)

From my oasis I ignored
Their plight, pretended
Everyone escaped. Lotte and Liesel
Did. They've spent their lives
Remembering the final sleep
Of murdered classmates.

Those classmates
Repeatedly ignored
By gods who were asleep
And leaders who pretended
Should have had a normal life
Like Lotte and Liesel.

Lotte and Liesel and the whole class
Endangered through pretence
     and ignorance
In my forgotten former life, asleep.

HIGH HOLY DAY

On Yom Kippur I feel
left out.
People around me
are dressed up.
So are their children's dolls.
I light a candle, don't
fast, see *Dallas*.

The leaf I touch has not
yet turned. Will next year's
earth be safe?
All this is written down
and sealed today.

I'm thinking of the girl
in the photo
(the mother-in-law I never knew)
deported to a Polish ghetto.
Did she learn to pray
or die for a religion
she did not believe in?

No lake to throw my sins into
only stirred up circles
in the puddle
of pale leaves shining
like injured angels.